AUG   2018

D1518542

SAFE ON YOUR

BIKE

PowerKiDS
press
New York

ROSEMARY JENNINGS

Published in 2017 by The Rosen Publishing Group, Inc.
29 East 21st Street, New York, NY 10010

Copyright © 2017 by The Rosen Publishing Group, Inc.

All rights reserved. No part of this book may be reproduced in any form without permission in writing from the publisher, except by a reviewer.

First Edition

Editor: Theresa Morlock
Book Design: Reann Nye

Photo Credits: Cover (background), 24 (pedals) tomertu/Shutterstock.com; cover (child), p. 1 Kim Reinick/Shutterstock.com; p. 5 Pressmaster/Shutterstock.com; p. 6 Hola Images/Getty Images; pp. 9, 24 (helmet) michaeljung/Shutterstock.com; p. 10, 24 (handlebars) Julia Kuznetsova/Shutterstock.com; pp. 13, 24 (handlebars) VectorLifestylepic/Shutterstock.com; pp. 14 Shliakhtun Volha/Shutterstock.com; p. 17 by John Carleton/Moment Select/Getty Images; p. 18 Inti St Clair/Blend Images/Getty Images; p. 21 Lina Arvidsson/Maskot/Getty Images; p. 22 AE Pictures Inc./DigitalVision/Getty Images.

Cataloging-in-Publication Data
Names: Jennings, Rosemary.
Title: Safe on your bike / Rosemary Jennings.
Description: New York : PowerKids Press, 2017. | Series: Safety smarts | Includes index.
Identifiers: ISBN 9781499427844 (pbk.) | ISBN 9781499428681 (6 pack) | ISBN 9781499429961 (library bound)
Subjects: LCSH: Cycling–Safety measures–Juvenile literature. | Bicycles–Safety measures–Juvenile literature.
Classification: LCC GV1055.J46 2017 | DDC 796.6028'9–dc23

Manufactured in the United States of America

CPSIA Compliance Information: Batch #BW17PK: For Further Information contact Rosen Publishing, New York, New York at 1-800-237-9932

CONTENTS

We ride bikes.

6

We are safe!

Helmets keep our heads safe.

9

Pads keep our knees safe.

Keep your hands on
the **handlebars**!

13

14

Keep your feet on the **pedals**!

Always watch for cars.

17

We stay out of the street.

We see people walking.
We ring our bells!

22

We love our bikes!

WORDS TO KNOW

handlebars

helmet

pedals

INDEX

WEBSITES

Due to the changing nature of Internet links, PowerKids Press has developed an online list of websites related to the subject of this book. This site is updated regularly. Please use this link to access the list: www.powerkidslinks.com/safe/bike

24